D0611431

The Little Book of

Lap Dogs

The Little Book of

Lap Dogs

WILLOW CREEK PRESS

© 2005 Willow Creek Press

Published by Willow Creek Press, P.O. Box 147, Minocqua, Wisconsin 54548

All rights reserved. No part of this book may be reproduced or transmitted in any form by any means, electronic or mechanical, including photocopying, recording, or by any information storage and retrieval system, without written permission from the Publisher.

Editor/Design: Andrea K. Donner

Photo credits:
p.2 © RonKimballStock.com; p.6 © M. Gunther/PeterArnold.com; p.7 © Jean-Paul Ferrero/Ardea.com; p.8 © Carol J. Kaelson / AnimalsAnimals; p.9 © Jean Fogle; p.11 © Barbara von Hoffmann / AnimalsAnimals; p.12 © Norvia Behling; p.13, 14 © Sharon Eide/Elizabeth Flynn; p.16 © Ulrike Schanz / AnimalsAnimals; p.17 © Norvia Behling; p.18 © Cheryl A. Ertelt; p.19 © Jean Fogle; p.20 © Bonnie Nance; p.21 © Close Encounters of the Furry Kind; p.23, 24 © RonKimballStock.com; p.25 © Sharon Eide/Elizabeth Flynn; p.27 © RonKimballStock.com; p.28 © Cheryl A. Ertelt; p.30 © Norvia Behling; p.31 © Sharon Eide/Elizabeth Flynn; p.32 © Norvia Behling; p.33 © Jean Fogle; p.34 © Jean-Michel Labat/Ardea.com; p.36 © Cheryl A. Ertelt; p.37 © RonKimballStock.com; p.38 © Jean Fogle; p.39 © Norvia Behling; p.41 © Werner Layer / AnimalsAnimals; p.42 © Gerard Lacz / AnimalsAnimals; p.44 © Norvia Behling; p.45 © Cheryl A. Ertelt; p.46 © Tara Darling; p.47, 48 © Norvia Behling; p.50 © RonKimballStock.com; p.51 © Tara Darling; p.53, 54 © Sharon Eide/Elizabeth Flynn; p. 55 © Norvia Behling; p.56 © Close Encounters of the Furry Kind; p.57 © Tara Darling; p.58 © Robert Pearcy/AnimalsAnimals; p.59 © RonKimballStock.com; p.61 © Cheryl A. Ertelt; p.62, 63 © RonKimballStock.com; p.64 © Close Encounters of the Furry Kind; p.65 © Jean Fogle; p.66 © Bonnie Nance; p.67 © Jean Fogle; p.68 © Norvia Behling; p.69 © Tara Darling; p.70 © Norvia Behling; p.72 © Bill Coster/Ardea.com; p.73 © Norvia Behling; p.74 © John Daniels/Ardea.com; p.75 © Tom & Dee Ann McCarthy/Unicorn Stock Photos; p.76 © John Daniels/Ardea.com; p.77, 78 © RonKimballStock.com; p.79 © Close Encounters of the Furry Kind; p.80 © Jean Fogle; p.81, 82 © Norvia Behling; p.83 © Bonnie Nance; p. 84, 85 © Tara Darling; p.86, 87 © Close Encounters of the Furry Kind; p.88 © Jean Fogle; p.89 © Bonnie Nance; p.90 © Sharon Eide/Elizabeth Flynn; p.92 © RonKimballStock.com; p.93 © Close Encounters of the Furry Kind; p.94 © Cheryl A. Ertelt; p.95, 96 © Sharon Eide/Elizabeth Flynn

Printed in Canada

My little dog—a heartbeat at my feet.

—Edith Wharton

Each body

has its art . . .

—Gwendolyn Brooks

A sound mind in a sound body is a short but full description of a happy state in this world.

—John Locke

Choose rather to be strong
of soul than strong of body.

—Pythagoras

The body says what words cannot.

—Martha Graham

What counts is not
necessarily the size of the dog
in the fight; it's the size of the
fight in the dog.

—Dwight D. Eisenhower

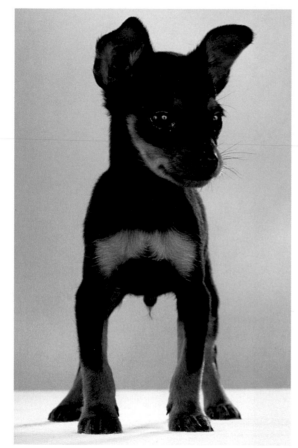

One drop of water helps to swell the ocean; a spark of fire helps to give light to the world. None are too small, too feeble, too poor to be of service.

—Hannah More

Small

opportunities are
often the beginning
of great enterprises.

—Demosthenes

We can do no great things;
only small things with great love.

—Mother Teresa

$\mathcal{R}$emember
there's no such thing
as a small act of
kindness. Every act
creates a ripple with
no logical end.

—Scott Adams

Great opportunities to help others
seldom come, but small ones surround us every day.

—Sally Koch

The smallest good deed is better than the grandest intention.

—Anonymous

I hope if dogs ever take over the world, and they choose a king, they don't just go by size, because I bet there are some Chihuahuas with some good ideas.

—"Deep Thoughts" by Jack Handy

A pekingese is not a pet dog;
he is an undersized lion.

—A.A. Milne

Even the tiniest Poodle or Chihuahua
is still a wolf at heart.

—Dorothy Hinshaw Patent

I know that dogs are pack animals, but it's difficult to imagine a pack of standard poodles... and if there was such a thing as a pack of standard poodles, where would they rove to? Bloomingdale's?

—Yvonne Clifford

If you look
good and dress well,
you don't need a
purpose in life.

—Fashion consultant
Robert Pante

I'm tired of all this nonsense about beauty being only skin-deep. That's deep enough. What do you want, an adorable pancreas?

—Jean Kerr

If you are
not in fashion, you
are nobody.

—Lord Chesterfield,
letter to his son,
April 30, 1750

Style is knowing
who you are, what
you want to say and
not giving a damn.

—Gore Vidal

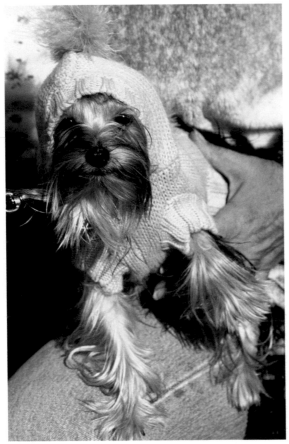

A chic type,
a rough type, an
odd type—but
never a stereotype.

—Jean-Michel Jarre

You know what charm
is: a way of getting the
answer yes without having
asked any clear question.

—Albert Camus

I never saw an ugly thing in my life: for let the form of an object be what it may——light, shade, and perspective will always make it beautiful.

—John Constable

There is no excellent beauty that hath
not some strangeness in the proportion.

—Sir Francis Bacon

Like anyone else, there are days I feel beautiful and days I don't, and when I don't, I do something about it.

—Cheryl Tiegs

I base my
fashion taste on
what doesn't itch.

—Gilda Radner

A truly elegant taste
is generally accompanied with
excellency of heart.

—Henry Fielding

The main source
of our wealth is goodness.

—Alfred A. Montapert

Without a rich heart, wealth is an ugly beggar.

—Ralph Waldo Emerson

There is no wealth
but life.

—John Ruskin

The ideals which have lighted my way, and time
after time have given me new courage to face life cheerfully,
have been *Kindness*, *Beauty*, and *Truth*.

—Albert Einstein

The finest qualities of our nature, like the bloom on fruits, can be preserved only by the most delicate handling.

—Henry David Thoreau

Let grace and
goodness be the
principal loadstone
of thy affections.

—John Dryden

There is nothing stronger
in the world than gentleness.

—Han Suyin

Happiness is the spiritual experience of living every minute with love, grace and gratitude.

—Denis Waitley

The most precious gift we can offer others
is our presence. When mindfulness embraces
those we love, they will bloom like flowers.

—Thich Nhat Hanh

A friend is one to whom you can pour out the contents of your heart, chaff and grain alike. Knowing that the gentlest of hands will take and sift it, keep what is worth keeping and with a breath of kindness, blow the rest away.

I think dogs are the most amazing creatures; they give unconditional love. For me they are the role model for being alive.

—Gilda Radner

The dog was created specially for children.
He is the god of frolic.

—Henry Ward Beecher

$\mathcal{D}$ogs are not our whole life, but they make our lives whole.

—Roger Caras

The fidelity of a dog is a precious gift demanding no less binding moral responsibilities than the friendship of a human being. The bond with a dog is as lasting as the ties of this earth can ever be.

—Konrad Lorenz

Call it a clan, call it a network, call it a tribe, call it a family. Whatever you call it, whoever you are, you need one.

—Jane Howard

Dogs are our link to paradise. They don't know
evil or jealousy or discontent. To sit with a dog on a hillside
on a glorious afternoon is to be back in Eden, where
doing nothing was not boring——it was peace.

—Milan Kundera

Money will buy you a pretty good dog,
but it won't buy the wag of his tail.

—Unknown

A man's soul can be judged by
the way he treats his dog.

—Charles Doran

Acquiring a
dog may be the
only opportunity a
human ever has to
choose a relative.

—Mordecai Siegal

Life's greatest happiness is to be convinced we are loved.

—Victor Hugo

Whoever said you can't buy happiness
forgot about little puppies.

—Gene Hill

Scratch a dog and you'll find a permanent job.

—Franklin P. Jones

$\mathcal{D}$ogs feel very
strongly that they
should always go
with you in the car,
in case the need
should arise for
them to bark
violently at nothing
right in your ear.

—Dave Barry

$\mathcal{A}$ good dog
deserves a good bone.

—US Proverb

If there are no dogs in Heaven, then when
I die I want to go where they went.

—Unknown

A dog owns nothing, yet is seldom dissatisfied.

—Irish proverb

The dog represents all that is best in man.

—Etienne Charlet